Praise for
Wise Older Woman
Growing in Grace and Sass

"I know of no other book which addresses in such an uplifting way the changing identity issues women face as we age. I know that many of my clients will find that this book provides an extremely helpful and encouraging perspective on becoming older."

–Susan Maxwell, Ph.D., Clinical Psychologist

"Debra Metelits has given us a treasure. Full of inspirational thoughts and documented quotes, exquisite and fanciful illustrations, and guided breathing affirmations, this work clearly reflects the enlightened spirit of the author. In our harried and stress-laden lives, we can take a few minutes to savor a page of this book and be transported to a place where age, wealth, even physical disability do not matter, for she guides us to our souls. Treat yourself to this jewel."

–Judith C. Engelman, M.D.

Diplomate of the American Board of Psychiatry and Neurology

Host of the former KFNX 1100 AM program
"Dr. Judy Is In: Psychiatry for Everyday Living."

"Metelits' words reflect the wisdom of a gentle healer. Each entry invites the reader to engage in a mini therapy session—with one's self as therapist and client—offering an affirming, energizing invitation for powerful daily transformation. The writing is playfully insightful. A beautiful book which made me want to shout, 'I am woman, hear me roar!'"

–Shana Helmholdt, Ph.D., Clinical Psychologist

"A great compilation of work on women's aging processes. A wonderfully positive and refreshing outlook based on centuries of thought from various cultures."

–Sonia Godbole, M.D., Psychiatrist

Clinical Assistant Professor, University of Arizona College of Medicine

Wise Older Woman:
Growing in Grace and Sass

Debra Metelits

To Joel,
whose love gives me wings

Acknowledgments

Thank you to each of you who has supported my journey in birthing this book. Thanks to the many writers and artists who not only gave permission for their work to be shared, but who also gave me their blessings for this project.

To my family—Joel, Ben, and Rachel—who gave me countless loving boosts literarily, technologically, and psychologically. Not only did they never reveal any boredom when their questions about my day inevitably resulted in my intricately detailed accounts of "Where I am in the Book Process"—they never failed to lovingly keep asking me about my day! To Max the Dog, whose deep, contemplative sighs and silent support always gave me comfort.

To those special women whose own stories and words I have included: Sandy Lovejoy, Sheila Paige Roth, Ruth James, Sandy Lewis, and Joan Lowell. To so many boosters of my spirit, especially Penny Altman, Sue Gonzales, Morgan Tripp, and Rachel Mandel. To Rabbi Sarah Leah Graftstein for help in research. To each of the literati in the book club. To my brilliant and scrupulous editor, Daria Ovide, who frequently pushed me further than I thought I could go, and thus made the book even better. To my always-patient, talented graphic artist Peri Miller, who not only designed a breathtaking cover, but taught me a lot about gentle breathing affirmations. To the immense artistic gifts and emotional support of Jack Wien. To Trishna Rodriguez, smartest (in intelligence and style!) computer guru.

And, most especially, to the support of my loving Higher Power, who not only tapped Sarah on the shoulder in her elder years with a wonderful surprise, but also me...

Table of Contents

Wise Older Woman: Growing in Grace and Sass

Dearest Fellow Traveler,

Welcome to a celebration of life and of you! I hope the following readings will help support your sacred transition to becoming an ever-more wonderful, Wise Older Woman.

To help subdue my own mounting anxiety about becoming an older woman, I began to collect affirming quotations. I wrestled—and later danced!–with questions about what aging would hold for me. While on this journey, I discovered so many delicious gems that I wanted to share them with you, my sister-traveler.

I found laughter, comfort, and inspiration in a wide range of sources: from diverse and ancient religious traditions to contemporary comedians; from a scientist to social activists; from a poet laureate to a nursery rhyme. All of these sources point to the wondrous opportunities that aging offers: the chance to come to peace with our unique life-histories; the chance to treat all parts of ourselves as precious, including our changing bodies; the chance to deliberately choose optimism and a gentle sense of humor; the chance to experience a heightened ability to perceive the sacred in everyday life; the chance to grow interpersonally; the chance to live more authentically by transcending limiting social norms about aging and women; and the chance to envision our spirituality as more loving and broad than ever before.

Each entry is offered as an emotional vitamin, a positive affirmation for the week or day, and a reminder to you of your precious value in a world in which it is not always easy to remember that you are a wonderful and Wise Older Woman! This collection is both a book and a workbook in which you are invited to read, to write, and to play!

The spiraling path of time may well bring us some challenges. But it also comes with great potential to surprise, awaken, and liberate us! As we free ourselves from the shackles of ageism and heal ourselves from self-limiting messages of shame about becoming older women, we blossom into elders who shine special light upon what it means to be truly human.

May you be abundantly blessed as you are led on your own unique journey to becoming a Wise Older Woman who embodies Radiant Light, Evolved Grace—and more than just a touch of Earthy Sass!

Good Journey!

Just the Sea and Me

While I am nervously adjusting a towel over my swimsuit for maximum thigh coverage, a woman at the beach suddenly catches my eye. A tall woman, she stands looking out to the sea. Amid many tanned, toned, scantily-clad bodies, she is wearing a faded tank suit which fits snugly over her protruding belly and a large, floppy, flowered hat. She appears to be in her mid-eighties.

Here is what startles me: despite her rounded belly, her thin, stork-like legs, and her out-of-fashion hat, she looks more dignified, grounded, and majestic than all those moving quickly around her. She gazes out to the horizon where small children, screaming with pleasure, race in and out of the ebbing waves. Are they her own grandchildren or great-grandchildren, or simply beautiful Young Children? With my eyes fixed on her, I feel at one with every creature at the shore, both under and out of the water. I suddenly throw off my cover-up and run, laughing, into the waves.

For today,
I release all self-consciousness.

I gently turn my attention to my breathing.
I deeply breathe in; I deeply breathe out.

You are invited to repeat the following breathing affirmation as many times as you wish in order to feel the truth of these words in your heart-space.

Breathing in, I think: *I am grounded* ...
Breathing out, I think: ... *and majestic*.

Not Again!

OH NO! Not another learning experience!

–Bumper sticker

I rarely have placed a bumper sticker on my car. But this one I found irresistible, and I smile at its message almost every day. For while I intellectually do believe that the goal of my life is to trust more in the spiraling path of spirituality and growth, my initial response to an upcoming "learning experience" is similar to the above quote: Run away! My first reaction is generally to fear change. I smile at my refrigerator magnet that proclaims: "Change is good. You go first!"

To the wise advice to "let go," I am in the camp of people who have never given up anything that didn't have my claw marks scratched on it. I don't want to give up a relationship, even if it is unhealthy. I don't want to give up control of an outcome that I desire. I don't want to change as I age. I don't want to ever feel disorientation or grief. Yet my wisest self knows that it is through such learning experiences that I become more insightful and grounded—a tree with roots so deep in the earth that my highest branches can gracefully dance in the wind.

As Sufi poet Rumi wrote in the thirteenth century: "We can let the circumstances of our lives harden us so that we become increasingly resentful and afraid, or we can let them soften us, and make us kinder. We always have the choice."

For today,
I am learning to embrace more new experiences with serenity.

I gently turn my attention to my breathing.
To help my heart-space open more, I lengthen my spine,
which allows me to sit a little taller.
I deeply breathe in; I deeply breathe out

You are invited to repeat the following breathing affirmation as many times as you wish in order to feel the truth of these words in your heart-space.

Breathing in, I think: *I am open* ...
Breathing out, I think: ... *to growing*.

The Imperfectly Perfect, Wonderful You

It is better to live your own destiny imperfectly
than to live an imitation of somebody else's life with perfection.

–Bhagavad Gita

The following story is often told of the great Rabbi Zusha of Hanipol, who lived in the late 1700's in Eastern Europe. When Rabbi Zusha lay crying upon his death bed, his students pleaded with him, "Dear Rebbe, why are you so sad? After all the good deeds you have done, surely you will merit a great reward in heaven!" "I'm afraid," said Zusha, "because when I get to heaven, I know that God is not going to ask me, 'Zusha, why were you not more like Moses?' I know that God is not going to ask me, 'Zusha, why were you not more like King David?' But I am afraid that God might ask me, 'Zusha, why were you not more like Zusha?!'"

To manifest our own unique essence in our lives is both a challenge and an opportunity. It is tempting to blame any inauthentic behavior on the expectations of our parents, the expectations of our spouse, or the expectation of our grown children. But, much as we love these dear ones, it is not really our primary business what they think of us. It is our business to be the most authentic individuals that we can be. Whenever we become aware that our actions are based on fear rather than authenticity, we can instead choose to risk being our unique, possibly eccentric, perfectly imperfect, fallible but lovable selves.

For today,
I choose the paths that most express who I really am.

I gently turn my attention to my breathing.
I deeply breathe in; I deeply breathe out.

You are invited to repeat the following breathing affirmation as many times as you wish in order to feel the truth of these words in your heart-space.

Breathing in, I think: *I am* ...
Breathing out, I think: ... *imperfectly perfect!*

A Nursery Rhyme Re-Visited

The Bold Woman Who Lived in a Shoe

There was a bold [old] woman who lived in a shoe,
She had many children and knew what to do.
"You are all lovable with special gifts," she said,
She hugged them all fondly and tucked them in bed.

–Diane Loomans, Karen Kolberg and Julia Loomans,
from *Positively Mother Goose*

What a delightful reversal this is of the traditional rhyme about that other, punitive woman who also lived in a shoe!

We start forming our ideas about age and gender when we are very young, and among the early influences are nursery rhymes and fairy tales. As adults, we have the power to re-imagine any shaming story in our lives, from traditional tales of our culture to negative spins we may have placed on parts of our own life-stories.

Access your power to re-create your reality by writing your life-story in your mind as what celebrated author Gail Sheehy describes as a "progress story" that focuses on growth, rather than as a "decline story" that focuses only on loss. One technique that can help you is using positive affirmations. When you become aware of a negative thought about yourself, change it into a positive thought, and write it down in the positive form. Even if you don't yet believe the positive words you have written— especially if you don't yet believe them!—repeating your new positive thought can have a powerful healing effect. Tape affirmations on your mirror and doorposts so that you are nourished by them frequently.

For today,
I choose only positive thoughts to feed my precious mind.

I gently turn my attention to my breathing.
I deeply breathe in; I deeply breathe out.

*You are invited to repeat the following breathing affirmation as many times as
you wish in order to feel the truth of these words in your heart-space.*

Breathing in, I think: *I can transform negative thoughts* …
Breathing out, I think: … *into positive thoughts.*

You Can Change the World

Be the change you wish to see in the world.

–Mahatma Gandhi

In 1890, the Butterfly Effect was first described. This is the theory that the universe is such an intricately interconnected web that a tiny change in one part of the universe can bring about rippling, unforeseen, ultimately huge effects in other parts of the world. The flap of a butterfly's wings in Brazil might eventually set off a tornado in Texas! Likewise, our smallest changes in self-affirmation and self-love can set off a ripple of effects that we would never predict.

I don't have to wait for the world to change to feel valued as an older woman. I can envision a world in which a woman's worth does not depend on her physical status, a world in which a man's worth does not depend upon his financial status, and a world in which an older person is revered for her experience and wisdom. As John Lennon reminded us, if we can only "imagine" a more evolved world and act as if it were true, we can help manifest it into reality. I believe that the world is actually changed—even if just a bit—because of changes within me.

For today,
I see myself as the Goddess and Webmaker
described by many cultures in the following words:
"She changes everything she touches,
and everything she touches is changed."

I gently turn my attention to my breathing.
I deeply breathe in; I deeply breathe out.

You are invited to repeat the following breathing affirmation as many times as
you wish in order to feel the truth of these words in your heart-space.

Breathing in, I think: *I am the change* ...
Breathing out, I think: ... *I wish to see*.

Yin and Yang

Life is a wonderful school.
Life is a mother------.

Can both of these statements be true? The daughter of an old vaudeville performer told me that these two sayings were her father's guiding principles in life. Sometimes one is true, sometimes the other is true, sometimes both are true simultaneously! Aging, for example, is a school in which we can learn humility, self-acceptance, and the sacredness of the present; but at times, aging can bring disheartening losses.

Often long-enduring intimate relationships grow so deeply that the two elders become inextricably, beautifully inter-connected and inter-dependent. This is the kind of love attributed to A.A. Milne's character Winnie the Pooh, who wistfully shares with Christopher Robin: "If you live to be a hundred, I want to live to be a hundred minus one day so I never have to live without you." But if one spouse declines or dies, the remaining partner is left with a loss that is almost unimaginable: the yin of excruciating absence, the yang of magnificent love.

As we move into older age, we are likely to find ourselves slowing a bit, along with a growing awareness that our time on Earth is not infinite. These changes often contribute to an even-deeper appreciation of the trembling beauty of the present. A baby—always a welcome sight—may now appear more miraculous and holy than ever before. Yet when we are most evolved in our mindfulness and patience, we might struggle physically to pick the baby up, to chase on our knees after the crawling toddler, or to toss the little one into the air: the yin of frustrating physical limitations, the yang of an ever-deepening reverence for life.

Aging can be bittersweet, or even an annoying or painful "mother------!" Yet if I am open to its lessons, aging is also a powerful catalyst in which I can grow into a more evolved, delight-filled, and complete human being.

For today,
I open my heart to the wisdom of Rumi:
"God turns you from one feeling to another
and teaches by means of opposites,
so that you will have two wings to fly, not one."

I gently turn my attention to my breathing.
I deeply breathe in;
I deeply breathe out.

*You are invited to repeat the following breathing affirmation as many times as
you wish in order to feel the truth of these words in your heart-space.*

Breathing in, I think: *Aging is the Yin* ...
Breathing out, I think: ... *Aging is the Yang*.

You are a Spiritual Being

We are not so much physical beings having a spiritual experience as we are spiritual beings having a physical experience.

–Pierre Teilhard De Chardin

The word "spiritual" does not necessarily mean "religious." For some of us, religion is a significant aspect of our spirituality; for others, it is not. What I mean by "spiritual" is soul-ful: a sense of being connected to the universe and a trust that there is something wondrous that is greater than oneself, whether that something is God, Highest Self, Nature, Healing, Wholeness, Creativity, Ultimate Reality, Love, Growth, Higher Power, Inner Child, or Inner Elder.

If we were simply physical beings who were having spiritual experiences, that would be a blessing in itself. But how much more empowering and uplifting to see ourselves primarily as *spiritual* beings having physical experiences. Some of these physical experiences are quite challenging; as Bette Davis once wryly commented: "Being old is not for sissies!"

For today,
I remind myself that the metaphysical aspects of my Self are even deeper,
more real, and more profound than my physical aspects.

I gently turn my attention to my life-giving breath.
I deeply breathe in; I deeply breathe out.

You are invited to repeat the following breathing affirmation as many times as you wish in order to feel the truth of these words in your heart-space.

Breathing in, I think: *My very essence* ...
Breathing out, I think: ... *is spiritual*.

Fertility of Mind and Soul

When Sarah, the first matriarch of the Jewish people, was close to ninety years old, God told her that she would at last have a baby. Sarah laughed.

–Adapted from Genesis 18:12

Is Sarah's laughter an expression of confused nervousness? Is it a laughter of rebellious disbelief? I like to think it is the deep-throated laughter of sheer surprise and delight that the Universe could still provide Sarah with fertility—her dearest wish—at such an advanced age.

Sarah is a role model of the fertility latent in our elder years—perhaps not the same fertility that gives us babies, but the fertility of ideas and creativity and leadership that sometimes blooms lushly when a woman has the solitude and independence of maturity, loosened from prior responsibilities to family. Anthropologist Margaret Mead noted that across cultures, older women often reveal a freeing of energy which she described as an unexpected and exuberant "post-menopausal zest."

I love that Sarah's response to news of her fertility is laughter, for humor is one of my most effective coping mechanisms. I've even added "Sarah" to my Hebrew name to remind myself that I can still be surprised and delighted by the Universe—and by my own abilities. If you feel moved to add or change any part of your name to something more fitting to the Authentic You, I encourage you to do it!

For today,
I am open to my continuing fertility of ideas, of curiosity,
and of creativity.

I gently turn my attention to my life-giving breathing.
I deeply breathe in; I deeply breathe out.

You are invited to repeat the following breathing affirmation as many times as you wish in order to feel the truth of these words in your heart-space.

Breathing in, I think: *I am fertile* ...
Breathing out, I think: ... *always*.

Metamorphosis

Just when the caterpillar thought life was over, she became a butterfly.

–Anonymous

Aging sometimes seems like it might be one of these caterpillar phenomena: many of us feel frightened about what is ending and are unable to foresee any metamorphosis into even modestly-colored moths! And yet social scientists have consistently been observing in middle-aged and older women an invigorating burst of self-confidence, optimism, and creativity. As seasoned women of middle and older age, many of us have undergone an experience like this, when the threat of an ending actually opened into a brighter vista than we had imagined possible.

Gail Sheehy, author of *Passages: Predictable Crises of Adult Life*, was hailed as a visionary in 1976 when she wrote about the developmental milestones and emotional challenges of adults in their twenties to late forties. When Sheehy aged twenty more years, however, she realized with surprise and delight that she and others her age were *still* growing and evolving dramatically. "It's embarrassing to admit, but in *Passages* I stopped delineating the stages of adult life at fifty," she observed. "How quaint that now seems!" To remedy this omission, in 1994 Sheehy created *New Passages*, a book in which she describes the rich potential inherent in the "Flaming Fifties" through the "Wisewomen in Training Sixties" and up to the "Celebratory Centenarians."

Sheehy no longer sees age forty-five as the end of adult psychological growth. Instead, she heartily invites us to celebrate age forty-five as the "infancy of a vast Second Adulthood." In this Second Adulthood, a woman has the chance to release limiting inhibitions, express her authentic voice, and do whatever nurtures her unique soul.

Just for today,
I spread my wings and embrace the new opportunities
of my vast Second Adulthood.

I gently turn my attention to my breathing.
I deeply breathe in; I deeply breathe out.

You are invited to repeat the following breathing affirmation as many times as
you wish in order to feel the truth of these words in your heart-space.

Breathing in, I think: *I am a Divine* ...
Breathing out, I think: ... *work in progress*.

Celebrating Authenticity

We learn to become female impersonators around adolescence,
and don't become free again until after menopause.

–Gloria Steinem

If we were fortunate when we were young, we were the little girls wearing ballet tutus with combat boots; flinging off scratchy crinolines to snuggle into soft overalls; wearing our hair braided one day, and allowing it to flow in a wild tangle the next.

As we grow into womanhood, we often get diverted from our natural selves as we are trained—by magazines, TV, film, and even by other women—to become acutely self-conscious of what is expected and appropriate and desirable in a female. We may swallow the idea that the most ideal woman is thin, young, white, and self-negating; we may then become more motivated by external approval than we are by our own authenticity.

These pressures erode our innate self-confidence and force us to become "female impersonators" striving to achieve unrealistic representations of female beauty. Naomi Wolf, author of the now-classic *The Beauty Myth*, observes a profound truth: "To airbrush age off a woman's face is to erase women's identity, power, and history . . . We as women are trained to see ourselves as cheap imitations of fashion photographs, rather than seeing fashion photographs as cheap imitations of women."

Have you ever noticed a gathering of middle-aged women, all dressed in purple with flamboyant red hats? They are part of the Red Hat Society, an organization for women age fifty and above who want to age with "verve and élan." They have taken their wardrobe cues from Jenny Joseph's famous poem "Warning." In the poem, the middle-aged narrator warns society that when she is old enough, she will then allow herself to do and wear whatever she wants, even if it is sporting a vivid purple dress with a delightfully mis-matched red hat. Wearing purple and red may not express the authentic You, but you *do* know what makes you feel beautiful and strong!

For today,
I delight in celebrating my authentic female self,
my authentic female body,
and my authentic choices about my appearance.

I gently turn my attention to my breathing.
I breathe in deeply; I breathe out deeply.

*You are invited to repeat the following breathing affirmation as many times as
you wish in order to feel the truth of these words in your heart-space.*

Breathing in, I think: *I confidently appear* ...
Breathing out, I think: ... *however I wish*.

Crowned with Silver

Crown me with wrinkles and gray hairs.

–Request made by Abraham to God
from Biblical retelling by Dayle Friedman

Wow, that request for the ornamentation of wrinkles and gray hair is probably not a prayer heard a lot today!

An ancient tale tells that Abraham was often frustrated with how often he was mistaken for his son Isaac. Abraham asked God to give him distinguishing markings so that others would know to respect him as the revered elder he was.

We live, though, in an ageist society, which means that elders are often marginalized or are looked upon with fear as a predictor of a diminishing future. It is easy to resign oneself to the idea that this attitude has always been present and will always be present. However, this would be incorrect.

Rabbi Zalman Schachter-Shalomi—a pioneer in aging who studied extensively with the Dali Lama, Jesuit priests, and Sufi mystics—helps us trace the origin of ageism. In ancient Biblical times, the elders of the tribe were deeply revered as collectors of wisdom and as advisors about matters both secular and sacred. However, the classical Greek ideal of beauty as only a youthful attribute strongly influenced the modern Western world. Furthermore, the Industrial Revolution and the more recent Technological Revolution also eroded the historical tradition of turning to elders for wisdom.

Elders are held in high esteem, though, in some Native American, Asian, African, and Aboriginal communities. Can we bring back the ancient appreciation of elders to our contemporary American society?

We must start with honoring ourselves. With so many of us Baby Boomers coming into our maturity now, we have a chance to act upon some of our unconventional, metaphysical values to transform the way aging is experienced: perhaps we will develop consciousness-raising groups for women about aging; perhaps we will choose to live in communal settings that we all help run; perhaps we will bring a stronger emphasis to quality of life over quantity of life. As the prophet Hillel said over two thousand years ago, "If we are not for ourselves, who will be for us? If we are only for ourselves, what are we? If not now, when?"

Just for today,
I feel a connection to the visionary elders of the past,
the present, and the future.

I gently turn my attention to my breathing.
I deeply breathe in; I deeply breathe out.

*You are invited to repeat the following breathing affirmation as many times as
you wish in order to feel the truth of these words in your heart-space.*

Breathing in, I think: *I am* ...
Breathing out, I think: ... *an esteemed elder*.

Your Ever-Growing Voice

I didn't have a voice until I was forty.

–Attributed to Virginia Woolf

Even the literary genius Virginia Woolf felt that her real voice—her honest self-awareness and confidence to express that genuine self—did not emerge until she reached mid-life.

Similarly, the famous suffragette and abolitionist Susan B. Anthony revealed that as a young woman, she was at first too timid to speak at rallies. But in later life, she reflected: "The older I get, the greater power I seem to have to help the world; I am like a snowball: the further I am rolled, the more I gain!"

Many of us are preoccupied in our earlier years with expressing only those parts of ourselves that we think will meet the approval of our parents, our peers, or our partners. It may not be until mid-life that we have energy and time to nurture our own voices. Besides Virginia Woolf, Susan B. Anthony, Rosa Parks, "Grandma" Moses, May Sarton, Eleanor Roosevelt, and many other artists and activists, think of the many middle-aged comedians—Roseanne, Mae West, Whoopi Goldberg—whose true voices of earthiness and humor did not mature until later in life. As Maggie Kuhn, leader of the Gray Panthers, used to exhort: "Stand before the people you fear and speak your mind—even if your voice shakes."

Just for today,
I honor my own voice, whether it is joyfully warbling off-tune,
howling in pain at a loss, or protesting forcefully against a social injustice.

I gently turn my attention to my breathing.
I softly release my jaw so that there is a small space
between my upper and lower teeth.
I deeply breathe in; I deeply breathe out.

You are invited to repeat the following breathing affirmation as many times as you wish in order to feel the truth of these words in your heart-space.

Breathing in, I think: *My voice* ...
Breathing out, I think: ... *is growing*.

You Are a Miracle

There are two ways to live: you can live as if nothing is a miracle—
or you can live as if everything is a miracle.

–Albert Einstein

One might think that a scientist of Einstein's stature would only value theories and facts that he could prove scientifically. Yet this brilliant intellectual was able to experience child-like awe and spiritual wonder about the many miracles and mysteries of everyday life. I am always brought back to a centered, spiritual place by another wonderful axiom of Einstein's: "Not everything that can be counted counts, and not everything that counts can be counted."

The years of life can be counted. But how wonderful that the ultimate reality of our lives—our spiritual, unique essence—cannot be quantified. No other human being has the exact same memories or experiences or insights that I have. My precious worth cannot be limited or expressed by any number—be it a salary, a weight on a scale, or a birthday.

For today,
I remember that I am a miracle.
I fly freely beyond any finite numbers.

I gently turn my attention to my breathing.
I deeply breathe in; I deeply breathe out.

You are invited to repeat the following breathing affirmation as many times as you wish in order to feel the truth of these words in your heart-space.

Breathing in, I think: *My worth* ...
Breathing out, I think: ... *is infinite*.

Your Precious Body

The Last Will and Testament of This Woman

To every woman who is my daughter
To every woman who is my sister:

I will to you first of all, my diets—
my grapefruit diet, my orange diet, rice diet, wine diet, water diet,
banana diet and fasting diet . . .

. . . I will you TOPS clubs, Weight Watchers Clubs, Pill Pushing
Doctors, amphetamines, water pills, thyroid pills, and laxatives
that I have known and I have known many— . . .

. . . I will you my douche bag
filled with lemon flavored scents,
mint flavored scents,
flower flavored scents,
washed rinsed and flushed with flavored scents.

I will you all the foams and jellies and sprays
and suppositories that I was ever
tempted to insert into that most mysterious warehouse of undesirable
smell.
I give you them all.
I give you them all . . .

. . . I give you every ad I ever read
that made me think I needed these things.

I will to you every bit of shame I ever was made to feel
about being the woman I was born to be.

I will you all of this
in the hopes that once you have all these things
you will realize that you don't need them
much sooner than I realized that.

—Claire Braz-Valentine

This brilliant poem is a direct and powerful reminder of how strongly we can feel pressure to define our femaleness in ways of which society approves. Implicit in these self-negating customs are hidden messages that our female bodies are somehow dirty, excessively wild, and in need of containment.

How freeing to be reminded that we actually need none of these straitjackets! In this will, we are entrusted with a true legacy in the narrator's intimate sharing of her own struggles. We are the fortunate heirs to her priceless, mature insights about our bodies' total innocence.

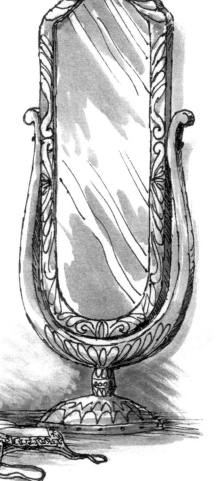

For today,
I offer to my daughters the role model
of a woman who is comfortable in her natural
female body.

I gently turn my attention to my breathing.
I picture myself naked before a beautiful,
gilded, full-length mirror.
I imagine gazing at myself with tenderness.
I deeply breathe in; I deeply breathe out.

*You are invited to repeat the following breathing
affirmation as many times as you wish in order to feel
the truth of these words in your heart-space.*

Breathing in, I think: *My entire body* ...
Breathing out, I think: ... *is lovable*.

Phenomenal You

Phenomenal Woman

Pretty [young] women wonder where my secret lies.
I'm not cute or built to suit a fashion model's size
But when I start to tell them,
They think I'm telling lies.
I say,
It's in the reach of my arms,
The span of my hips,
The stride of my step,
The curl of my lips.
I'm a woman
Phenomenally.
Phenomenal woman,
That's me . . .

. . . Men themselves have wondered
What they see in me.
They try so much
But they can't touch
My inner mystery.
When I try to show them,
They say they still can't see.
I say,
It's in the arch of my back,
The sun of my smile,
The ride of my breasts,
The grace of my style.
I'm a woman
Phenomenally.
Phenomenal woman,
That's me . . .

– Maya Angelou

How delicious that the narrator of this poem is a middle-aged woman who confidently sings of her sexuality. As we age, we need not become neutered.

For some of us, aging may bring a new ability to say no to sexual behavior we do not desire. Others of us will want to continue our enjoyment of, and reverence for, our erotic selves. We may want to use traditional or alternative medicine to enable us to do so. Some of us may find sexual satisfaction in ways we had not considered before—in a relationship with a different or younger partner, for example, or in pleasuring ourselves.

Even if we do not desire sexual contact, our bodies still need to be affectionately touched. Three hugs per day is a minimum!

For today,
I feel comfortable with my sensuality and free to enjoy it.

I gently turn my attention to my breathing.
I deeply breathe in; I deeply breathe out.

You are invited to repeat the following breathing affirmation as many times as you wish in order to feel the truth of these words in your heart-space.

Breathing in, I think: *I am* ...
Breathing out, I think: ... *phenomenal*.

She Rises

The following picture is from Shiloh Sophia McCloud's delightfully engaging *Color of Woman: A Coloring Book and Journal*. This image, entitled "She Rises," depicts what I imagine the spirit of "Phenomenal Woman" would look like if we could see that spirit manifested. I love her full hips, power, grace, and lightness. Her lovely wings look as if they shortly will bear her aloft!

When I asked McCloud for permission to use her art in my book, she wrote back to me: "Yes. Yes! The answer is always yes!" In that wonderful reply, I could imagine McCloud's face tilted back, the wind dancing in her long hair, and a sense of almost contagious optimism. Feel free to decorate "She Rises" by playing with collage, stickers, markers, colored pencils, or any medium that catches your fancy!

Launching Loved Ones

Three men were arguing about when life begins. The first man said that life begins at the moment when the sperm meets the egg. "No," countered the second man, "life begins when the child draws his first breath outside of the womb." The third man disagreed with them both: "Life begins when the children move out of the house and the dog dies!"

–Anonymous

Even as we smile at this old joke, we can probably guess that it was created by a man. For women especially, empty-nest syndrome can be triggered when our child initially leaves home or when he "boomerangs" back and leaves again. This life-cycle event evokes our great elation and pride in our child's independence, perhaps mixed with some degree of grief and disorientation about our own status and meaning. Over many decades and many life-cycle events, I have felt comforted and uplifted by the following poem. The poet speaks to our initial fear—and later, our profound joy— about our children's steps away from us, and their steps forward onto their own journeys.

Bon Voyage
Someone I know is going away.
I was thinking about how I don't want him to go,
and how it is sad to be left behind.

Then I found a card.
There is a beach in the foreground
with huge tracks like a land machine's
going down toward the sea.

At the end of the tracks is no land machine,
but after all a huge turtle
just heading into the sea—
the endless sea that stretches before him.

So this card calls to mind the fact that
where the land ends and the sea begins
the turtle ceases to be a grave, ungainly
plodding creature,
and becomes something graceful and free
that can go on effortlessly forever.

Inside the card said: **Bon Voyage**
which, it suddenly came to me,
means **Good Seeing!** —

not traveling from this place to that
and leaving anyone behind—just a **Good Seeing**.

He was going to sea—going to **see**.
And right here so am I.
And right there so are you.
And everywhere so are our children.

Beneath the greeting the card said:
(And don't forget to write).

Bon Voyage!
Good seeing good!

–Polly Berrien Berends

For today,
I bless all those that I have helped launch. Letting them go in this non-
possessive, loving spirit is the way that God nurtures and launches us all
into new pathways. As you enter a new stage of life, listen to your Higher
Power lovingly whispering to you: "Bon Voyage! Good seeing good!"

I gently turn my attention to my breathing.
I deeply breathe in; I deeply breathe out.

*You are invited to repeat the following breathing affirmation as many times as
you wish in order to feel the truth of these words in your heart-space.*

Breathing in, I think: *Good* ...
Breathing out, I think: ... *seeing good*.

The First Generation

Proclaim liberty to the next generation! We . . . are the first generation of women to enter our mature years after the modern women's movement.

–Maria Harris

We can easily take for granted the strides in women's rights tirelessly gained over the last forty years of the feminist movement, the "second wave" feminism of the 1970's and 1980's. We must recognize and protect our rights while continuing to stride forward—for equal pay for equal work, for an end to rape and rape culture, for girls' education at home and in the developing world.

For the sake of our daughters, our granddaughters, and our "surrogate" daughters (women emotionally but not biologically connected to us), Christian theologian Maria Harris urges us to be the women we authentically are: the feisty, empowered women we discovered ourselves to be through the modern feminist movement. The younger generations need us to model for them the dignity and pride of older women accepting themselves lovingly. Young women are watching us as we journey through the labyrinth of time, and they need to draw on our courage to transcend the unrealistic societal expectations they face now and the ones they may have to face in the future. We can't always be perfect, but we can always provide stepping stones of strength.

We can empower young women to continue becoming feminists who wish every person a liberation from constricting ideas, especially artificial ideas about gender and age. We can empower young people to journey, as the Psalmist says, "from strength to strength."

For today,
I honor the women warriors of the past, present, and future.

I gently turn my attention to my breathing.
To help me feel even more grounded to the Earth and to my roots,
I allow my hands to rest on my lap. My palms face downwards,
one hand on each thigh.
I breathe in deeply; I breathe out deeply.

You are invited to repeat the following breathing affirmation as many times as you wish in order to feel the truth of these words in your heart-space.

Breathing in, I think: *From strength* ...
Breathing out, I think: ... *to strength*.

Seeding the Garden of Life

I actually got to experience a bit of treasured "seeding" from Rabbi Zalman Schachter-Shalomi when I was a young mother. It was transformational. Schachter-Shalomi was already silver-haired and exuded an aura of dignity and wisdom. (Thank goodness that I did not realize what a world-acclaimed scholar he was, or I would have been much more abashed.)

I was at a small gathering at a home where each participant was being given the high honor of reading directly from an ancient Torah scroll which had reverently been laid out on a table adorned with lace tablecloths and flowers. I was frantically hiding behind pillars and people because I was the only one there who could not read a word of Hebrew. Rabbi Schachter-Shalomi ultimately spotted me and beckoned me forward. Face burning, I whispered to him that I knew no Hebrew. Instead of simply dismissing me, he quietly and kindly responded, "Well then, today you will learn one Hebrew letter—the smallest letter in the alphabet—a *yud*."

He pointed to a *yud* in the scroll ... then another ... and another. "Now, do you think you can find one *yud* anywhere here?" I looked intensely at the squiggles of black, and I tentatively pointed to what I hoped was a *yud*. He smiled and said, "There, my child, you have just read from the Torah." My eyes brimmed with tears of relief, wonder, and awe.

Zalman Schachter-Shalomi was helping to seed my future with trust and confidence. Author of *From Age-ing to Sage-ing: A Profound New Vision of Growing Older*, he defines "seeding the future" as a sacred process that we elders can do when we harvest our life knowledge and trust that we will keep flowering as long as we plant seeds in others. Sometimes the young are aware that they are thirsty for our input; sometimes we may need to simply plant seeds that will flower later. But the modern world has an emptiness, warns Schachter-Shalomi, that can only be healed by connecting with the accumulated wisdom of elders—elders who tend to see themselves as guardians of both future generations and of Mother Earth.

Just for today,
I experience myself growing and enriching this planet.

I gently turn my attention to my breathing.
I deeply breathe in; I deeply breathe out.

You are invited to repeat the following breathing affirmation as many times as you wish in order to feel the truth of these words in your heart-space.

Breathing in, I think: *I am seeding the future*...
Breathing out, I think: ... *with great love*.

Becoming Who She Is

The following picture is, for me, an uplifting expression of Schachter-Shalomi's vision of "seeding the future." In Shiloh Sophia McCloud's inspired drawing, "Becoming Who She Is," a woman's spirit allows itself to draw from the Earth's fertile abundance of musky leaves and flowers to nourish branches that grow outward from her torso. These branches will in time become solid, sheltering trees.

I love how this beautiful woman, by letting herself become who she really is, connects deeply to the past, the present, and the future. Enjoy coloring her however you wish, feeling free to write words of hope, wishes, or gratitude anywhere on the picture.

Look What Came Today: A Present!

Yesterday is history.
Tomorrow is mystery.
That's why they call today the gift of the "Present."

–Anonymous

As we age, some of us fall prey to anxiety or pessimism about the future. Many philosophers believe that a great deal of this worry stems from difficulty in living fully in the present.

I once had a mentor to whom I would frequently fret over some problem. She would respond to me in a voice I thought was genuinely puzzled, "Now, when is this thing going to happen?" I would reply with well-justified self-pity and irritation, "I said it could happen in a month." "Now, Debra," she would say in the same gentle voice, "tell me again when this is going to happen?" We might go back and forth like this a few times until I would finally surrender to what I knew she was pointing out: whatever I was fretting about was *not* today. I needed to change my attitude so that I could truly live "One Day at a Time."

In *Fierce with Reality* (such an aptly named anthology about aging!), Gerry Berg and Sally Gadow make a striking observation about the link between living in the present and healthy aging. They point out that time seems to have two dimensions: duration and density. Ironically, "it is only when the aspect of duration of time is seen not to be endless that we fully recognize the aspect of depth, or density, of time." This new perception of the density of time allows us to enjoy the present all the more intensely.

For today,
I appreciate that the present is always
fresh and alive with potential.

I gently turn my attention to my life-giving breathing.
I deeply breathe in; I deeply breathe out.

*You are invited to repeat the following breathing affirmation as many times as
you wish in order to feel the truth of these words in your heart-space.*

Breathing in, I think: *Today is* ...
Breathing out, I think: ... *a gift*.

The Zen of Time

"There is more to life than simply increasing its speed."

–Mahatma Gandhi

This quote could certainly be claimed with pride by our pet tortoise! But these words have a lot of implications for us humans, too.

When Gandhi, father of modern India, first said these words, he was trying to motivate the people of colonial India to return to spinning cloth by hand. He wanted Indians to end the form of British colonial exploitation that forced peasants to import expensive cloth from the more speed-efficient mills of their overlords. Yet equally important to Gandhi was his wish for his people to embrace the spiritual truth that there is always "more to life than simply increasing its speed"—that there was beauty and dignity in traditional Indian spinning.

Gandhi's words also have meaning beyond their original historical context. His words apply to all of us who are practicing the art of aging with dignity. I once hiked up a steep mountain with a woman who was twenty-five years my senior. At first, I passed her, feeling slightly guilty that I was overtaking her but enjoying my speed. However, as we approached the summit, she passed me! She laughingly commented that she had found lately that she needed "to go slower to get higher." Like my friend, I too have found that I need "to go slower to get higher." When I am less frenzied in my daily activities, allowing myself more time to meditate, to enjoy Nature, to pray, and to play, I feel emotionally "higher."

Not all of us are changing our speed. Some of us are still running marathons; some of us are just beginning to train for marathons. But many of us will have noticed a bit of slowing in our pace, whether it is the length of our nightly bedtime preparations or the amount of time needed to summarize our medical history!

However, when we really come to believe that there is something more important in life than simply increasing its speed, we may find that we are also more open to giving our full, conscious, Zen-like attention to whatever wonders are right in front of us: the texture of a rock ... a budding rose ... the smile on a child's face.

For today,
I am deeply awake in the present.

I gently turn my attention to my breathing.
I deeply breathe in; I deeply breathe out.

*You are invited to repeat the following breathing affirmation as many times as
you wish in order to feel the truth of these words in your heart-space.*

Breathing in, I think: *My awareness* ...
Breathing out, I think: ... *is Zen*.

What is Your Glorious Age?

Aging to Westerners is a youth robber . . . , while to a Vietnamese, aging is a reward. This is reflected in our language: we Vietnamese often say I am given so and so number of springs when we tell our age . . . To live to old age is to be blessed by high Heaven— . . . So don't be shocked when you visit Vietnam and nine out of ten Vietnamese you meet ask you how old you are.

–Dahn Ho

Acclaimed author Maria Harris describes a similar custom in traditional Chinese practice "where visitors greet their hosts with the question, 'And what is your glorious age?' If the person questioned names an age greater [than forty], the visitor's face brightens with delight, shining with increasing intensity the higher the age reported."

These non-Western ways of talking about age are so different from our language customs surrounding age in America. I remember learning as a child that to be polite, "you should never ask a lady her age." And if a lady of any age over forty is asked, she should demurely and coyly reply, "Thirty-nine." Yet these customs of denying aging are obviously not the only reality; they are merely artifacts of our societal fear of aging. How affirming to be aware that in some traditions, information about longevity is openly solicited, acknowledged, and celebrated!

Now that we have attained the glorious age that we are, Maria Harris urges us to reflect on the following questions:

"Now that you have reached this glorious age, what do you wish to wear?"

"Now that you have reached this glorious age, what do you wish to tear up?"

"Now that you have reached this glorious age, what do you wish to create?"

For today,
I am grateful for the many springs I have been given.

I gently focus my attention on my breathing.
I deeply breathe in; I deeply breathe out.

*You are invited to repeat the following breathing affirmation as many times as
you wish in order to feel the truth of these words in your heart-space.*

Breathing in, I think: *My glorious age today* ...
Breathing out, I think: ... *is ⁓ years*.

The Magic of Crone-dom

A Crone is like you and me. What does set the Crone apart, however, is her willingness to tell the truth about her life. Crone women fly directly into the face of ageism and sexism. They refuse to be put down.

–Susan Ann Stauffer

The Virgin Maiden, the Mother, and the Crone are the trinity of the female in ancient Celtic lore. The word "crone" comes from the word "crown," indicating wisdom emanating from the head. Whereas the archetype of the crone probably connoted for our mothers a withered witch of a woman, some enlightened female elders today are self-identifying as crones, welcoming the beginning of this special phase of life, and re-appropriating the word "crone" to imbue it with its original and very positive meaning.

The crone has always symbolized female aging. But today, as in ancient times, she again represents an aging that is intense in vitality, abundant in wisdom, and experienced in independence. She is honored for the depth of her ability to empathize, the courage of her persistence, the perspective that only accumulated experience can offer, and the compassion that has been brewed and distilled over many years. Her magic comes from years of intimacy with both love and pain, births and losses. (Why, grandchildren certainly know the magic of Grandmother's hugs!)

For today,
I honor myself as a Wise Woman who has just a touch of wildness!

I gently turn my attention to my breathing.
I deeply breathe in; I deeply breathe out.

You are invited to repeat the following breathing affirmation as many times as you wish in order to feel the truth of these words in your heart-space.

Breathing in, I think: *I am beginning to embrace* ...
Breathing out, I think: ... *being a wise crone woman*.

Achieving Your Beautiful Face

Sometimes It's Easy

I used to laugh a lot
That's why my face is wrinkled
That's why my teeth are chipped
By sandy wind

Sometimes it's easy
Sometimes it's not so easy
Sometimes I feel like I can't go on

Then I remember
What really makes it easy
Being with you
When I'm singing my song

–Hoyt Axton

What evolved self-acceptance these lyrics celebrate! The singer has arrived at a truce with her changing body, even with her wrinkles. She acknowledges that life and aging are sometimes very challenging, yet she has discovered the balm to ease her pain: emotional intimacy with another person, and authentic self-expression through one's own song—whether that "song" is writing, telling stories, dancing, painting, quilting, or actually singing.

For today,
I am reminded of Eleanor Roosevelt's insight that a girl is *given* the face that she is born with, but the face of a mature woman is one that she *achieves*.

I gently turn my attention to my breathing.
I deeply breathe in; I deeply breathe out.

You are invited to repeat the following breathing affirmation as many times as you wish in order to feel the truth of these words in your heart-space.

Breathing in, I think: *I am evolving* ...
Breathing out, I think: ... *into my mature beauty*.

41

The Real You

The Skin Horse had lived longer in the nursery than any of the others. He was so old that . . . most of the hairs in his tail had been pulled out to string bead necklaces . . .

. . . "What is REAL?" asked the Rabbit one day, when they were lying side by side near the nursery fender, before Nana came to tidy the room. "Does it mean having things that buzz inside you and a stick-out handle?"

"Real isn't how you are made," said the Skin Horse. "It's a thing that happens to you. When a child loves you for a long, long time, not just to play with, but REALLY loves you, then you become Real."

"Does it hurt?" asked the Rabbit.

"Sometimes," said the Skin Horse, for he was always truthful. "When you are Real, you don't mind being hurt."

"Does it happen all at once, like being wound up," he asked, "or bit by bit?"

"It doesn't happen all at once," said the Skin Horse. "You become. It takes a long time. That's why it doesn't happen often to people who break easily, or have sharp edges, or who have to be carefully kept. Generally, by the time you are Real, most of your hair has been loved off, and your eyes drop out and you get loose in the joints and very shabby. But these things don't matter at all because once you are Real you can't be ugly, except to people who don't understand . . . Once you are Real you can't become unreal again. It lasts for always."

–Margery Williams,
from *The Velveteen Rabbit: Or How Toys Become Real*

Having one's hair loved off and one's joints change sounds a bit foreboding, but what value is there greater than being the REAL, authentic, one-of-a-kind you? The wise Horse observes that becoming REAL is a process partly dependent on aging, but which "doesn't happen often to people who break easily, or who have sharp edges, or who have to be carefully kept."

For today,
let me honor the REAL love that children and adults have for the REAL me.
Help me be a person who doesn't break easily, a person without sharp edges,
a person who doesn't have to be carefully controlling of others.

I gently turn my attention to my breathing.
I deeply breathe in; I deeply breathe out.

You are invited to repeat the following breathing affirmation as many times as
you wish in order to feel the truth of these words in your heart-space.

Breathing in, I think: *The REAL me* ...
Breathing out, I think: ... *is sacred*.

"I Hope You Dance!"

Dennis Deloria's famous photograph, entitled "Dancers of the Third Age," captures elders from Liz Lerman's Dance Exchange performing a scene from the ballet *Swan Lake*. It always evokes in me a smile of delight and an itch to get up and dance! This photo celebrates the dancer in every single one of us, and it celebrates feeling comfortable in our own skins. Inside each of us is an innocent Inner Child who does not age, an Inner Child who is an innate and creative dancer, an Inner Child who intuitively knows how to express feeling though movement, whether movement of sensuality, grief, or exuberance.

For today,
I joyfully embrace this ancient African proverb:
"If you can talk, you can sing. If you can walk, you can dance."

(And even if you can't walk, you can still dance in the inter-generational
Dance Exchange Company shown here! Wheelchairs are choreographed in
swirling patterns to accompany the dancers on foot, and expressive hand
movements are choreographed for those in wheelchairs.)

I gently turn my attention to my breathing.
I deeply breathe in; I deeply breathe out.

*You are invited to repeat the following breathing affirmation as many times as
you wish in order to feel the truth of these words in your heart-space.*

Breathing in, I think: *I say yes* ...
Breathing out, I think: ... *to life's invitations*.

You Are a Precious Child

You are a child of the universe,
no less than the trees and the stars.

–Max Ehrmann,
from "Desiderata"

Sometimes the idea of being a precious Child of the Universe is difficult to sustain. Unfortunately, too many of us suffer feelings of worthlessness, isolation, and shame. Perhaps we were raised with shaming messages from our family of origin; perhaps we have been swallowing oppressive messages from our society about aging women.

Today we make no place in our lives for shaming messages. Unlike shame, most emotions bring us a gift. When we feel anger, we know we need to make a change in ourselves or in our situation. Joy brings delight and gratitude. Pain brings with it the opportunity to heal. Loneliness lets us know we need to reach out more to others. Guilt lets us know we need to make amends to someone for something we did that went against our own values. The only useless emotion is shame: a feeling not that we *did* something wrong, but that *we ourselves* are wrong, useless, or damaged. I encourage you to join me in casting off as false any lingering feelings of shame.

For today,
I affirm that I am intrinsically innocent and good, a Child of the
Universe who is no less precious than the shimmering butterflies
or the endless mountains. I am no less majestic than a breaching
grandmother whale—an ancient whale covered in barnacles—and
still an innocent and magnificent child of The Divine.

I gently turn my attention to my breathing.
I deeply breathe in; I deeply breathe out.

*You are invited to repeat the following breathing affirmation as many times as
you wish in order to feel the truth of these words in your heart-space.*

Breathing in, I think: *I am a Child* ...
Breathing out, I think: ... *of the Universe*.

Welcoming Your Inner Elder

You will discover yourself embracing your inner elder with affection and
wisdom, even as you may have already embraced your inner child.

–Maria Harris

Maria Harris, internationally renowned educator, authored *Jubilee Time: Celebrating
Women, Spirit, and the Advent of Age.* She encourages us to listen to our precious
"Inner Child"—that perfectly innocent, playful, vulnerable Little One that lives on
inside of our psyches, no matter our age.

Harris encourage us as well to make space in our minds for the concept of our
precious "Inner Elder"—that Wise Older Woman who arrives in our psyche close to
our Jubilee year, our year of turning age fifty.

The Jubilee, which reoccurred every fifty years in ancient times, is described in the
Bibical chapter of Leviticus: "This fiftieth year is sacred. It is a time of freedom and of
celebration when all debts will be canceled and slaves will be freed to return home to
their families." Harris has evolved this idea of the holy, liberating Jubilee time for the
community to the idea of a holy, liberating Jubilee time for an individual woman. In
the Jubilee years of fifty and beyond, a woman can cancel shaming messages and free
herself and others from ageism and sexism.

As we enter our Jubilee, we begin learning to honor our Inner Elder—the
Compassionate Wise Old Woman, the Female Sage that exists within our minds.
Perhaps we picture this Inner Elder as our Future Self, when we are older and even
wiser and more compassionate than we are now. Perhaps we see her as a beloved
grandmother; perhaps we perceive her as the Madonna; perhaps we embrace her as
Shekinah, the Judaic female In-Dwelling Presence of God; or perhaps we envision her
as the Buddhist Kuan Yin, who extends not just two, but multiple, mothering arms to
protect and guide. Transcending any limiting norms of society, my Inner Elder offers
me a model of aging with inner power and radiance.

For today,
I begin to perceive, to connect with, and to trust my Inner Elder.

I gently turn my attention to my breathing.
To help me feel more receptive to the Universe,
I rest my hands in my lap.
My hands are cupped open, palms up to the Heavens.
I deeply breathe in; I deeply breathe out.

*You are invited to repeat the following breathing affirmation as many times as
you wish in order to feel the truth of these words in your heart-space.*

Breathing in, I think: *I am envisioning* ...
Breathing out, I think: ... *my Inner Elder*.

Healing in Her Wings

Inner Child, Inner Elder—come out and play! The following illustration, entitled "Healing in Her Wings," is from one of Shiloh Sophia McCloud's powerful coloring books for women. This drawing expresses just one of hundreds of ways to envision an Inner Elder.

Free free to write words on the page and to color part or all of it with colored pencils, watercolors, felt markers, or crayons. And, of course, feel happily free to color *far* outside the lines!

Surrendering What You Have Outgrown

... Be yourself ...
Take kindly to the counsel of the years,
gracefully surrendering the things of youth ...

–Max Ehrmann,
from "Desiderata"

It is our individual choice whether to color our hair or to opt for plastic surgery. The best choice for one woman may be the poorest choice for another. But we have all seen women who desperately grasp at youthful attributes beyond reasonableness. Very thin women of advanced age can be heard to be shaming themselves that they can't lose five more pounds; these women still embrace the false philosophies that a woman "can never be too rich or too thin," and that "a woman's main value lies in her appearance." Perhaps these women are afraid that they will be rejected by employers or even loved ones if they can't compete in appearance with younger women. Perhaps it is just too painful to let in the reality that they are aging.

We need to celebrate ourselves exactly as we are today, no matter what our age or hair color or texture of skin. As a friend of mine declares with a sense of abandon that I love: "If I want to, I shall paint my face with the rain and color my hair with the wind!"

For today,
I celebrate myself. Like a sea crab which has healthily outgrown its limiting shell,
I have outgrown all limiting societal "rules" that would suppress my True Self.

I gently turn my attention to my breathing.
I deeply breathe in; I deeply breathe out.

*You are invited to repeat the following breathing affirmation as many times as
you wish in order to feel the truth of these words in your heart-space.*

Breathing in, I think: *I gracefully surrender* …
Breathing out, I think: … *what I have outgrown*.

Planting Your Own Carob Tree

A young man came upon an eighty-year-old man planting a carob tree. "Old man," he questioned, "do you actually think you will be alive to see this tree bear fruit?" The old man answered, "When I came into the world, there were carob trees here for me and my children; I want there to be carob trees here for my grandchildren."

–Ancient Talmudic story

The old man in the story above knows that he will not live to see the little carob trees mature and flourish. But, as it is written in the thirteenth-century Judaic text *Ethics of our Fathers*, "Just because you cannot complete the task does not mean that you are free to not begin it." A stunning example of this determination are the deathbed words of suffragette Susan B. Anthony, who said about her as-yet-unfulfilled vision of women gaining the right to vote: "Failure is impossible." (Wow, what glorious words to go out on!)

The famed psychologist Erik Erikson believed that each stage of life presents its own potential for either growth or regression. In terms of aging, the negative options can result in a depressed self-absorption and "a sense of stagnation and boredom." However, on the positive side, aging presents the wonderful options of integrity— the acceptance of one's *whole* life, with its ups and downs—and of generativity—the opportunity to "pay it forward" to the next generation.

Erikson defines integrity as the "acceptance of one's one and only life cycle and of the people who have become significant to it as something that had to be . . . It thus means a new and different love of one's parents." This acceptance and forgiveness frees energy that previously might have been bound up in resentment or regret; this new energy is then free to flow into generativity.

For Erikson, generativity is the "concern for establishing and guiding the next generation." Generativity can be expressed in creative work that will be passed on to future generations, in mentoring a younger person, in nurturing grandchildren, or in helping to repair a broken world by working toward social justice. In fact, an elder friend, who retired from her work as an executive and who recently completed a tour of duty in the Peace Corps, shared that ten percent of Peace Corps volunteers are *over* age fifty!

Just for today,
I accept what I cannot change,
but I work with all my heart toward what can be changed.

I gently turn my attention to my breathing.
I breathe deeply in; I breathe deeply out.

You are invited to repeat the following breathing affirmation as many times as you wish in order to feel the truth of these words in your heart-space.

Breathing in, I think: *Today and tomorrow* ...
Breathing out, I think: ... *I am a planter of trees*.

Napping in God's Hands

It's not that I'm afraid to die,
I just don't want to be there when it happens.

–Woody Allen,
from *Death (A Play)*

The only Bible verse I memorized as a child was the Twenty-Third Psalm, and the following line always confounded me: "Yea, though I walk through the valley of the shadow of death, I shall fear no evil, for Thou art with me." It may sound crazy, but, even as an adult, my limited human mind actually wants God's assurance that no evil will occur because somehow I will cleverly evade death. However, the Psalmist cannot protect us from the eventuality of death. He can reassure us, though, of an enormous gift: we will be protected from evil. For me, evil is the illusion that I am unlovable.

Some of us look forward to an after-life; some do not. But, for all of us, what a comfort to know that our Higher Power is always nurturing, never punitive. What a blessing to be able to look at our increasing age not as a process to be marked by mocking black balloons at a birthday party, but simply as a phase of life: a phase with its own gifts and potentialities, just like every other phase.

For today,
I can peacefully nap in the hands of a nurturing God.

I gently turn my attention to my breathing.
I breathe in deeply; I breathe out deeply.

*You are invited to repeat the following breathing affirmation as many times as
you wish in order to feel the truth of these words in your heart-space.*

Breathing in, I think: *I relax with complete ease* …
Breathing out, I think: … *into God's hands*.

Anointed and Adored

Thou preparest a table before me in the presence of mine enemies;
Thou anointest my head with oil; My cup runneth over.

–Psalm 23

This verse brings back to me the memory of having tenderly massaged my infants' delicate, dry scalps with soothing baby oil. Being gently and respectfully anointed by another can still feel loving and healing when we are adults.

Some of us may feel undeserving of the gifts offered in the Psalm above. We may be embarrassed about hanging upper arms or dimpled thighs because we fear that they show our bodies are less worthy than those of the young. But the Psalmist is reassuring us that no matter what our age, weight, or gender, God is anointing our heads with oil, a ritual that was once reserved for honoring royalty. We are loved as if we were precious royalty, and the love is so abundant that our cups "runneth over."

Sometimes we actually need more than words. We really need tables laid out for us, even though the enemy is lurking; we need overflowing cups, reminding us that we are more than enough; we need the reverent caress of oil upon our skin from a Source outside of ourselves. We need these bodily affirmations of our worth, for the soul and the mind and the body are all interconnected.

Whether it is the mildly perfumed oil of a massage, the ruffling of our hair by an autumn breeze, an infant cuddled in our laps, or swimming naked in blue water, our bodies deserve daily attention, tenderness, and play.

For today,
I know that the Nameless One blesses all my endeavors to unite
Holy Spirit with Holy Body.

I gently turn my attention to my breathing.
I deeply breathe in; I deeply breathe out.

*You are invited to repeat the following breathing affirmation as many times as
you wish in order to feel the truth of these words in your heart-space.*

Breathing in, I think: *I am anointed* ...
Breathing out, I think: ... *and adored*.

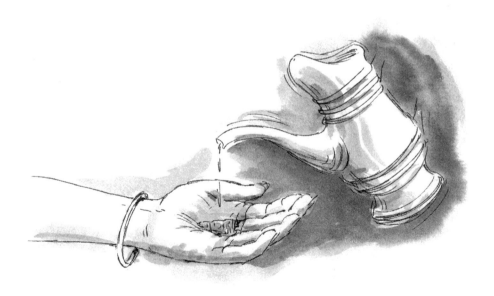

Eating Mangoes While Naked

"Eat Mangoes Naked" and be a "Succulent Wild Woman."

–SARK

What delicious, earthy, sensual images SARK offers in the titles of her many books, especially *Eat Mangoes Naked* and *Succulent Wild Woman*. No matter what your age or body shape, you can eat mangoes naked, savoring the fruit of the earth, as well as the fruit that is your body.

Emotional juiciness does not belong only to the young. Just as we roll and rub a lemon or orange to extract more juice from it, our bodies and psyches have been rolled and rubbed up against the challenges of life, but that only makes us more psychologically juicy!

For today,
I affirm that I am a juicy, "succulent wild woman."

I gently turn my attention to my breathing.
I deeply breathe in; I deeply breathe out.

You are invited to repeat the following breathing affirmation as many times as you wish in order to feel the truth of these words in your heart-space.

Breathing in, I think: *I am*...
Breathing out, I think: ... *a free, unbridled spirit*.

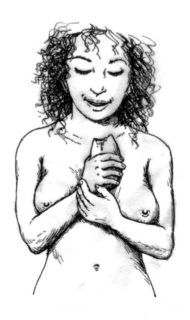

Your Real Beauty

The Rabbit sighed. He thought it would be a long time before this magic called Real happened to him. He longed to become Real, to know what it felt like; and yet the idea of growing shabby and losing his eyes and whiskers was rather sad. He wished that he could become it without these uncomfortable things happening to him.

–Margery Williams,
from *The Velveteen Rabbit: Or How Toys Become Real*

Ah, dear Rabbit, how we all wish that! If only we could gain the treasures of seasoned wisdom and insight without having any of our fur "loved off" (or darned extra fur added in different places!). Yet, like precious silver that changes over time from a harsh, glaring brightness to an elegant soft patina, our own patinas shine with increasing glow the older we become.

For today,
let me accept having a bit of my fur gently "loved off"
so that I may feel gloriously alive.

I gently turn my attention to my breathing
I deeply breathe in; I deeply breathe out.

*You are invited to repeat the following breathing affirmation as many times as
you wish in order to feel the truth of these words in your heart-space.*

Breathing in, I think: *My Realness* ...
Breathing out, I think: ... *is beautiful*.

Choosing Courage

Know! A person walks in life
on a very narrow bridge.
The most important thing
is not to be afraid at all
is not to be afraid at all.

–Rebbe Nachmann of Breslov

Reb Nachmann, a famous European rabbi of the nineteenth century, was devastated over the death of his young son. He worked hard to overcome his depression by consciously focusing on life-affirming thoughts like this one. This paradoxical quote is wonderfully expressive of the human condition: acknowledging the fragility of the bridge of human existence, it also urges us to walk that bridge with joy, trust, and faith. As Mark Twain wisely observed, courage is not the *absence* of fear; courage is traveling forward *despite* the fear.

For today,
when I choose to live in the sacredness of the present,
my courage and faith expand.

I gently turn my attention to my breathing.
I deeply breathe in; I deeply breathe out.

You are invited to repeat the following breathing affirmation as many times as you wish in order to feel the truth of these words in your heart-space.

Breathing in, I think: *In this sacred moment* ...
Breathing out, I think: ... *I am not afraid at all*.

Choosing Optimism

I'll tell you a little secret: I'm starting to get optimistic.

–Bessie Delany, age 101
from *Having Our Say: The Delany Sisters' First 100 Years*

What a mischievous and delightful closing sentence to centenarian Bessie Delaney's autobiography! At over one hundred years old, in a life beginning with her father born into slavery, Delany fought for many decades against prejudice, racism, and hatred.

How wondrous that this elder is growing more optimistic! In addition, she is grateful that she has succeeded in all she ever wanted: to be treated as an individual. "At least I'm sure that in the Lord's eyes, I am an individual," she says. "I am just me! The Lord won't hold [my looks] against me . . . because He made me that way! He thinks I am beautiful! And so do I, even with all my wrinkles! I am beautiful!"

It takes fierce courage to experience cruelty first-hand and still look into the future with growing optimism and with a basic belief in the goodness of most people. As the writer of Proverbs observes, it is a true "Woman of Valor"—like Delany—who "looks into the future and smiles."

For today,
I give thanks for unknown Blessings already on their way.

I gently turn my attention to my breathing.
I deeply breathe in; I deeply breathe out.

You are invited to repeat the following breathing affirmation as many times as you wish in order to feel the truth of these words in your heart-space.

Breathing in, I think: *I choose* ...
Breathing out, I think: ... *optimism*.

Healing Through Insight

Insight is always unlocking the gates of time.

–Interpretation of Geela Rayzel Raphael's
translation of "Maariv"

During the middle and later parts of our lives, we may have more time and motivation than ever before to use our emotional insight to review our past and come to terms with it. We understand that in every unresolved situation, the ultimate goal is forgiveness—but not one minute before we are truly ready to forgive.

Don't despair about mistakes you have made. We all have made mistakes! Remember that you can always make amends for any wrongdoing by apologizing, by changing your behavior, and by owning your mis-steps, even if the amends comes in the form of a letter you write to a deceased loved one. Because insight can unlock the gates of time, it is never too late to address any area in which we feel regret.

As the beloved nineteenth-century Reb Nachman of Breslov taught: "If you believe that you can damage, then believe that you can fix. If you believe that you can harm, then believe that you can heal." These words remind me of the hauntingly beautiful Native American teaching that when a person heals an emotional wound from the past, she automatically breaks up an entire cycle of dysfunction, for the healing mystically goes back seven generations, and the healing also goes forward seven generations, causing a cascading effect of positive change.

For today,
time is fluid as I experience insight.

I gently turn my attention to my breathing.
I deeply breathe in; I deeply breathe out.

You are invited to repeat the following breathing affirmation as many times as you wish in order to feel the truth of these words in your heart-space.

Breathing in, I think: *I send healing energy* …
Breathing out, I think: … *to the past and the future*.

To Everything There is a Season

To everything there is a season
And a time for every purpose under heaven:
A time for tradition, and a time for change;
A time to be alone, and a time to be together;
A time to be young , and a time to be old;
A time to begin monthly bleeding, and a time for it to end;
A time to be with women, and a time to be with men; . . .
A time to learn, and a time to teach;
A time to free oneself, and a time to share freedom with others . . .

–Anne Tolbert,
from "A Personal 'Seder' to Celebrate Aging"

How affirmed I feel that Tolbert adapts this sacred song of acceptance from Ecclesiastes to include "A time to be young, and a time to be old." I feel especially affirmed that she includes "a time to begin monthly bleeding, and a time for it to end" because, in doing so, she brings our female bodily changes into the realm of the Holy.

There are many books on the market for how to cope with some of the admittedly challenging biological accompaniments to menopause, as well as many jokes about the "power surges" of hot flashes and comic descriptions of peri-menopausal women—like the cartoon "Maxine"—as cranky but lovable.

But we are just beginning to recognize the sacredness of menstruation, that "Wise Wound," and we are just beginning to honor the sacredness of its conclusion. Our bodies do not just contain our souls: our bodies are soulful. When it comes time for the ending of menstruation, this will be a relief for some, a sorrow for some, and a bittersweet poignancy for others. But the ending of our ability to be biological mothers must not end the nurturing spirit within us, which can now be channeled more to our own growth and to the repair of a fractured world.

For today,
I remember that there is
a time for every season and every purpose
under Heaven.

I gently turn my attention to my breathing.
I deeply breathe in; I deeply breathe out.

You are invited to repeat the following breathing affirmation as many times as you wish in order to feel the truth of these words in your heart-space.

Breathing in, I think: *I deeply honor* ...
Breathing out, I think: ... *every season of my growth*.

Permission to Simply "Be"

We are not "human do-ings;" we are "human be-ings."

–Anonymous

"What do you do?" is one of the first questions you are likely to face at a dinner party. Sometimes we women are too self-effacing and reluctant to brag about our professional accomplishments. Sometimes we are sheepish about having had several different careers, when in reality these varied experiences add much texture and richness to our perspectives.

Yet sometimes, as we reduce or retire from "work," we feel ungrounded and disoriented. Our market-based society greatly values the "do-ing" of work for material achievements. Moreover, many of us have defined ourselves primarily as "do-ers" for others: for our husbands, our parents, our children, or our grandchildren. If we are not sacrificing to do something for someone else, are we still worthy?

I once read about a man who was a quadriplegic in a nursing home. He began getting very depressed, questioning his value because he felt he could do so little for himself or for anyone else. Then he had an uplifting awareness: by smiling and expressing thanks for each act of kindness that a nurse performed, including telling each nurse "May God bless you," he was "do-ing" a great deal.

In the inspired words of the Dalai Lama, "The planet does not need more successful people. The planet desperately needs more peacemakers, healers, restorers, storytellers, and lovers of all kinds."

For today,
I honor myself not just for what I "do"—but for "be-ing" aware, "be-ing" awake,
and "be-ing" part of the loving energy on Earth.

I gently turn my attention to my breathing.
I deeply breathe in; I deeply breathe out.

You are invited to repeat the following breathing affirmation as many times as you wish in order to feel the truth of these words in your heart-space.

Breathing in, I think: "*Simply "be-ing"* …
Breathing out, I think: … *is Holy*.

Honoring Even Uncertainty

In fact, this midlife anxiety [about] searching for answers to
the mysteries of life, death, and the meaning of existence .... is
exceedingly normal; people who profess to be spiritually *content* as
they enter midlife are generally sound asleep at the wheel.

–Kathryn Cramer, Ph.D.

What a relief to read this observation by noted psychologist Kathryn Cramer,
internationally recognized expert on the psychological effects of change and author
of *Roads Home: Seven Pathways to Midlife Wisdom*. Yes, there are many who stay in
denial as they age. Even though it is healthy and normal to process these existential
issues, it can also be frightening. Is there anybody who doesn't laugh in recognition
at Woody Allen's famous protest: "I don't want to achieve immortality through my
work, I want to achieve it through not dying!"

However, renowned aging expert Rabbi Zalman Schachter-Shalomi observes that
"people who cannot look ahead as they grow older *back* into the future, inexorably
moving onward in time without looking ahead." And if we are only backing into the
future, all we can see is our past, with little motivation to welcome the present and
the future.

For today,
I welcome becoming fully awake, even if that means awareness
of uncertainties about the future.

I gently turn my attention to my breathing.
I deeply breathe in; I deeply breathe out.

*You are invited to repeat the following breathing affirmation as many times as
you wish in order to feel the truth of these words in your heart-space.*

Breathing in, I think: *I honor reverently*...
Breathing out, I think: ... *even my questions*.

Not Curses, But Gifts

"But I don't want to be dependent on taking oxygen,"
groaned the eighty-four-year-old woman whose low oxygen was a
severe health risk for her. "Well," her physician gently smiled,
"then should we also take away your glasses, so that you don't get
dependent on them, either?"

–Anonymous

Some of us wail about the number of pills we have to take, or the fact that we need a grab bar in the bathroom, or a cane. Initially, it can certainly feel humbling and frightening to require medicine or equipment that we did not need previously. Yet medical supports are not curses to be endured: they are tools from God—gifts— to help us live each day as fully as possible. They ultimately make us not more dependent, but more independent.

Still, I have to admit I was shocked when the audiologist told me that I could benefit from hearing aids. "I'm too young to need those!" I whined at first. But when I received the hearing aids the following week, I proudly proclaimed to my children, "I am now bionically enhanced!" Today, I delight in hearing the soft snoring of my pup, every line in a movie, and the haunting "wuthering" of the tall trees before a storm.

For today,
I see medical supports as a gift from God
so that I can live the richest life possible.

I gently turn my attention to my breathing.
I deeply breathe in; I deeply breathe out.

*You are invited to repeat the following breathing affirmation as many times as
you wish in order to feel the truth of these words in your heart-space.*

Breathing in, I think: *I gratefully accept* …
Breathing out, I think: … *medical gifts*.

You Always Deserve Dignity

As I grow older, do not leave me;
As my strength ebbs, do not forsake me.

–Psalm 71:9

The Psalmist acknowledges the fear we may have about becoming more dependent on others as we move into advancing age. Some of us had secure childhoods and reassuring memories of being appropriately and healthily dependent as children. However, others of us had dysfunctional beginnings in which our vulnerability and dependence were treated as shameful and annoying. If our appropriate needs were treated as shameful when we were little, the thought of needing to depend more on others as we age is especially frightening.

If we need more help than we did when we were young, let us be drawn to generous-hearted helpers who treat us with the dignity and gentleness that we deserve. I once read of a son who carried a wheelchair down to the oceanside so that his mother could delight in the ocean spray that she loved; when I can conceive of being taken care of in this way, I feel courage and serenity. Even if our physical powers decline, we know that our spirituality can continually enlarge.

For today,
I make sure my needs are taken care of in respectful and honoring ways.
As I accept more help from others,
I can also lean more and more
on an unconditionally loving Higher Power.

I gently turn my attention to my breathing.
I deeply breathe in; I deeply breathe out.

You are invited to repeat the following breathing affirmation as many times as you wish in order to feel the truth of these words in your heart-space.

Breathing in, I think: *I always deserve* ...
Breathing out, I think: ... *unconditional love*.

Beyond Rubies

What is the value of a good woman?
Her price is beyond rubies.

Although this verse is generally thought of as a husband's loving tribute to his wife, the value for a woman of a good female friend is also beyond rubies. As an only child, I have always believed the saying that "a best friend is the sister that destiny forgot to give you." And, in addition, I have found that I seek communion with a circle of dear women around me.

The ancient Jewish text *Ethics of our Fathers* actually commands us to "acquire a friend" if we do not have one. Why would we be required to develop a friendship? Because it is easier to love humanity in the abstract than to do the occasionally ego-deflating repair work of friendship. (Remember Charlie Brown's woeful admission that he loved mankind, it was just people he found difficult?) The challenges of friendship include opening ourselves up enough to be intimate, owning our mistakes, and accepting others despite their inevitable flaws. All this soul work is completely worthwhile, though, for who else except a close friend can know when you're kidding yourself, can remind you of your past victories, and can genuinely believe in you when you temporarily cannot? Often our friends are angels withskin on.

For today,
I treasure my friendships with trustworthy, loving people.
Sometimes it is only through the voice of another human that I can
hear the Divine, Un-Nameable Spirit.

I gently turn my attention to my breathing.
I deeply breathe in; I deeply breathe out.

*You are invited to repeat the following breathing affirmation as many times as
you wish in order to feel the truth of these words in your heart-space.*

Breathing in, I think: *My value is* ...
Breathing out, I think: ... *beyond rubies*.

You Are a Vital Piece of the Whole

No man is an island,
Entire of itself.
Each is a piece of the continent,
A part of the main.
If a clod be washed away by the sea, Europe is the less.

–John Donne

This poignant passage by sixteenth-century Anglican priest and poet John Donne, written while he was close to death, illustrates his belief in the interconnectedness of all of life, a belief important to healthy aging. Becoming geographically isolated from loved ones, or actually losing them, can understandably lead to feelings of severe abandonment. That is why the awareness of your sacred interconnectedness with the world is so vital, especially in older age.

Rabbi Rami Shapiro describes a similar feeling about human interconnectedness, using the analogy of a jigsaw puzzle: "Every piece needs the whole for its integrity and coherence. And the whole needs each piece to fulfill its purpose and bring meaning and order to the puzzle. Once a piece is in its proper place, its separateness is surrendered. We know a piece is in its place when it blends with the whole and disappears . . . The mission of the individual is to take [her] place in the puzzle by letting go of the illusion of fragmentation."

When our unique piece of the puzzle of the universe blends with the whole and disappears, we know we are neither better than others nor less than others. We are each Children of the Universe; we each have a Divine right to be here.

For today,
I release the "illusion of fragmentation."
I celebrate that the unique me is essential to the world!
No matter what my situation, I can connect with others
through actions and prayers.

I gently turn my attention to my breathing.
I deeply breathe in; I deeply breathe out.

You are invited to repeat the following breathing affirmation as many times as
you wish in order to feel the truth of these words in your heart-space.

Breathing in, I think: *I am vital* ...
Breathing out, I think: ... ***to the integrity of the whole***.

The Power of Community

The following picture, excerpted from artist Klaus Holitzka's book *Power Mandalas*, is entitled "The Power of Community." Holitzka describes his goal in this mandala as the expression of each person's "connection to all human beings," the same idea expressed in the previous entry.

I like to think of this never-ending circle of dancing bodies being of different ages, places of origin, and religions. Holitzka suggests that you paint "the various people in the colors of the rainbow, or paint them in both wild and quiet color patterns." Have fun!

You Are a Masterpiece

Those whom the gods love grow young. It's true.
The gods love those who grow young because they have taken the
trouble to do so. The chronologically young is a given gift; growing
young into what is called old age is an achievement, a work of art.

–Anna Halprin

In Anna Halprin's view, growing young means deliberately staying open to life and its positive energies. It means moving our bodies in new ways, even if we initially feel self-conscious and timid. It means interacting with others, even if we feel like emotionally isolating. It means staying engaged with life rather than settling into a jaded boredom.

Halprin, a noted dancer, tells of the ardent hope of her father, Isadore. He yearned to dance once again with his beloved wife Ida at an upcoming event in the nursing home where they both lived. Isadore had been wheelchair-bound for the past three years, but, in preparation for this dance, he started stretching on a regular basis. On the night of the special event, Isadore "wheeled on stage, … managed to get out of his wheelchair, to stand up and to holler, 'Come on, Ida, let's dance!' … Not even Nureyev could have done a more astonishing and beautiful dance than Isadore and Ida Schuman, age ninety-four and eighty-nine." What Isadore and Ida had created was a masterpiece.

Just for today,
I celebrate that I am evolving into a masterpiece—
a magnificent work of art
shaped by my unique strengths, losses, resilience, and creativity.

I gently turn my attention to my breathing.
I deeply breathe in; I deeply breathe out.

You are invited to repeat the following breathing affirmation as many times as you wish in order to feel the truth of these words in your heart-space.

Breathing in, I think: *I am* ...
Breathing out, I think: ... *a work of art*.

Still Discovering

I refuse to tiptoe quietly through life, only to arrive safely at death.
I intend to slide in, thoroughly used up and yelling,
"Wow! What a ride!"

–Hunter S. Thompson

As we age, we do want to take extra care of our bodies, nurturing them with wholesome food, exercising them with sweaty pleasure, and following the medical advice of trusted health care providers. We want to use our bodies for appreciating the cool spring breeze, for enjoying the animal strength in our limbs, for hugging our partner or grandchild or kitten.

But we may also want to take our bodies on adventures beyond what they are used to! As Mark Twain so wisely advised: "Twenty years from now you will be more disappointed by the things you didn't do than by the ones you did. So throw off the bowlines. Sail away from the safe harbor. Catch the trade winds in your sails. Explore! Dream! Discover!"

Consider expanding the goals on your "bucket list" to include some that you might not have allowed yourself previously. Stroll around your back yard naked! Begin taking belly dancing lessons! Get your hands smeared with color as you create your first painting! Buy lubrication and a personal massager unlike any you've ever seen before! Sink your hands into rich mud as you help build a life-giving fish pond in a village in Cameroon! Visit Australia even though none of your friends wants to go! Let yourself laugh so hard you almost pee! Parasail high in the sky through a cloud!

Just for today,
I allow myself to experience moments of bliss.
When life is painful, I still show up, despite the challenge.
When life is glorious, I noisily drink in life's wonders,
including the wonder of me!

I gently turn my attention to my breathing.
I deeply breathe in; I deeply breathe out.

You are invited to repeat the following breathing affirmation as many times as
you wish in order to feel the truth of these words in your heart-space.

Breathing in, I think: *I am open to*...
Breathing out, I think: ... *discoveries of joy*.

Daughters and Mothers

If it's not one thing, then it's your mother.

–Robin Williams, comedian

This quip always makes me smile, although I know it is not applicable in all situations. Sometimes mothers do get stuck with unfair blame for causing all of our problems, a situation I understood with much more empathy when I myself became one! Yet, our mothers' reactions to growing older often serve as role models that we follow, either consciously or unconsciously. Some of our mothers' reactions to aging might be inspiring, while others might increase our anxiety.

Wise author Maria Harris encourages women who have achieved their Jubilee—their fiftieth year and beyond—to reflect on the following thought-provoking questions:

"Describe your mother's adult life after age fifty. What was the Jubilee like for her?"

"What have been/were your mother's greatest joys?"

"What have been/were your mother's greatest sorrows?"

"How are you most like, and most unlike, your mother?"

"Giving yourself lots of silence in order to hear the answer, what are some things your mother wants to say to you, now that you are a Jubilee Woman?"

~~~~~~

~~~~~~

~~~~~~

~~~~~~

"What do you want to say to her?"

~~~~~~

~~~~~~

~~~~~~

~~~~~~

Just for today,
I draw upon the beauty of my mother's strengths. If my mother felt
pushed into self-destructive behaviors, I am able to release myself from
re-living those negative patterns. I embrace my right to healthfully and
consciously choose the thoughts and actions that will most enrich my
Jubilee years.

I gently turn my attention to my breathing.
To help me connect even more deeply to my mother-energy,
I place one hand gently on my belly.
I deeply breathe in; I deeply breathe out.

*You are invited to repeat the following breathing affirmation as many times as
you wish in order to feel the truth of these words in your heart-space.*

Breathing in, I think: *I bless* ...
Breathing out, I think: ... *my mother*.

Breathing in again, I think: *I bless* ...
Breathing out again, I think: ... *my precious self*.

83

A Visit to Your Inner Elder (Tea and Cookies Optional!)

> Elders are *not* 'senior citizens' who get gold watches at retirement, move to Sunbelt states, and play cards, shuffleboard, and bingo ad nauseam . . . Elders . . . are wisdomkeepers . . . By an act of faith, they can say, 'For the benefit of who we are and what we may become, it's good to experience old age.'
>
> –Zalman Schachter-Shalomi

Rabbi Zalman Schachter-Shalomi urges us to notice how dramatically different the words "elderly" and "elder" sound. The first word, "elderly," brings to mind being frail and passive; the second word, "elder," connotes being treated with the dignity and respect that many traditional cultures have long reserved for their most experienced, honored mentors and guides.

Schachter-Shalomi urges us to work on nurturing a relationship with our Inner Elder through a meditation such as the one that he created on the next page. Allow yourself to take a few deep breaths. You are now being invited on a gentle journey to visit the Even More Evolved You of the Future.

Journey to Your Future Self

Sit quietly . . . as you become calm and centered. For a few moments, follow the inflowing and outflowing of your breath.

Then count slowly from your actual age up to the number 120, which is described in the Bible as the Age of Accomplished Wisdom. Visualize in your mind's eye walking up a set of stairs leading to the door of your Inner Elder. When you knock on the door, your Realized Self—the embodiment of boundless compassion and wisdom—greets you with a warm embrace. As you gaze into your Inner Elder's eyes, you feel unconditionally loved and reassured about your progress so far.

As a pilgrim confronting the highest, most all-embracing source of wisdom, feel free to ask your Inner Elder for guidance about an issue that you have been puzzling over . . . When you receive your answer, rest in silence for a while. If no clear answer comes, then trust that it will come with time.

Now, as you look again into the eyes of your Enlightened Self, receive these words of encouragement: "Journey on with confidence and with blessings as you proceed on your path. Visit me again whenever you would like."

Just for today,
I trust the Inner Elder within me for guidance and wisdom.

I gently re-focus my attention on my breathing.
I deeply breathe in; I deeply breathe out.

You are invited to repeat the following breathing affirmation as many times as you wish in order to feel the truth of these words in your heart-space.

Breathing in, I think: *I honor* ...
Breathing out, I think: ... *my Inner Elder*.

Go Forth on the Quest

In Genesis 12:1, during Abraham's seventy-fifth year of life, God tells him to go with his wife to the land of Canaan, to leave all of the life he has known and start on a brand new path. In Hebrew, God's words to Abraham—"Lech L'cha"—have often been translated as "Go forth to a land that I will show you." Renowned scholars Rabbi Arthur Waskow and Rabbi Phyllis Berman offer what I believe is the most profound translation: "Walk forth by going more deeply into yourself—to a land that I alone, God alone, can make visible to you."

We may have a hard time imagining being called upon to go on a quest at the age of seventy-five. (Especially if we don't even have the destination in our GPS!)

But actually, aren't we all called to go on a quest in middle and older age? Aren't we all called to a journey with many unknowns, to a journey that will probably take us more deeply into our spiritual selves, to a place we may not know yet? In Genesis, God does not promise to take Abraham on a regressive journey that will bring him back to a younger age; God beckons Abraham to a land so special that he has not been able to see it before!

One might think that at seventy-five, very little personal growth remains to be developed. But this passage suggests just the opposite. It declares that God has a spiritual harbor to show us that we can only find by trusting more deeply our own internal compasses, which will lead us to come to peace with our unique life histories, to bring ourselves to forgiveness, and to treat all parts of ourselves as precious.

It is not just Abraham who received a call from God to go on a quest in later age. We are each blessed to go on a spiraling quest that will demand persistent optimism, a ready sense of humor, a heightened ability to see the sacred in everyday life, and a courageous commitment to never-ending growth.

For today,
I trust that my own quest will take me
deeper and deeper into an understanding of
what it means to be human in this world.

I gently turn my attention to my breathing.
I deeply breathe in; I deeply breathe out.

*You are invited to repeat the following breathing affirmation as many times as
you wish in order to feel the truth of these words in your heart-space.*

Breathing in, I think: *I embrace* ...
Breathing out, I think: ... *my unique quest*.

Works Cited

All images, unless noted otherwise, are original illustrations by Jack Wiens. www.jackwiens.com.

A Nursery Rhyme Re-Visited (P. 6-7)

Loomans, Diane, Karen Kolberg, and Julia Loomans. "The Bold Woman Who Lived in a Shoe." *Positively Mother Goose*. Tiburon, CA: H. J. Kramer/Starseed Press, 2001. P. 1.

Sheehy, Gail. *New Passages: Mapping Your Life Across Time*. New York: Ballantine, 1995. P. 172.

Metamorphosis (P. 14-15)

Sheehy, Gail. *Passages: Predictable Crises of Adult Life*. New York: Ballantine, 2006. P. xxii.

---. *New Passages: Mapping Your Life Across Time*. New York: Ballantine, 1995. P. xxi, xxiv-xxv, 7, 172.

Celebrating Authenticity (P. 16-17)

Steinem, Gloria. "Gloria Steinem: A Profile." *On Women Turning 50: Celebrating Mid-Life Discoveries*. Cathleen Rountree. New York: HarperCollins, 1993. P. 139.

Wolf, Naomi. Introduction. *On Women Turning 50: Celebrating Mid-Life Discoveries*. Cathleen Rountree. New York: HarperCollins, 1993. P. 2.

Crowned with Silver (P. 18-19)

Friedman, Dayle. "Crown Me with Wrinkles and Gray Hair: Examining Traditional Jewish Views of Aging." A *Heart of Wisdom: Making the Jewish Journey from Midlife Through the Elder Years*. Ed. Susan Berrin. Woodstock, VT: Jewish Lights, 1997. P. 5.

Schachter-Shalomi, Zalman and Ronald Miller. *From Age-ing to Sage-ing: A Profound New Vision of Growing Older*. New York: Grand Central/Hachette, 1995. P. 60-64.

Your Precious Body (P. 22-23)

Braz-Valentine, Claire. "The Last Will and Testament of This Woman." *On Women Turning 50: Celebrating Mid-Life Discoveries*. Cathleen Rountree. New York: HarperCollins, 1993. P. 21-23.

Phenomenal You (P. 24-25)

Angelou, Maya. "Phenomenal Woman." *Phenomenal Woman: Four Poems Celebrating Women*. New York: Random House, 1994. P. 4-5. Originally printed in *And Still I Rise* by Maya Angelou. New York: Random House, 1978.

She Rises (P. 26-27)

McCloud, Shiloh Sophia. "She Rises." *Color of Woman: A Coloring Book and Journal*. Berkeley, CA: McCloud Press, 2004.

Launching Loved Ones (P. 28-29)

Berends, Polly Berrien. "Bon Voyage." *Whole Child/Whole Parent*. New York: Harper & Row, 1983. P. 345.

The First Generation (P. 30)

Harris, Maria. *Jubilee Time: Celebrating Women, Spirit, and the Advent of Age*. New York: Bantam/Random House, 1995. P. 78-79.

Seeding the Garden of Life (P. 31)

Schachter-Shalomi, Zalman and Ronald Miller. *From Age-ing to Sage-ing: A Profound New Vision of Growing Older*. New York: Grand Central/Hachette, 1995. P. 53, 187, 211-213.

Becoming Who She Is (P. 32-33)

McCloud, Shiloh Sophia. "Becoming Who She Is." *Color of Woman: A Coloring Book and Journal*. Berkeley, CA: McCloud Press, 2004.

Look What Came Today: A Present (P. 34-35)

Berg, Geri and Sally Gadow. "Toward More Human Meanings of Aging." *Fierce With Reality: An Anthology of Literature on Aging*. Ed. Margaret Cruikshank. Topsham, Maine: Just Write Books, 2006. P. 225.

What is Your Glorious Age? (38-39)

Ho, Dahn. "Old Age in Vietnam." *Fierce with Reality: An Anthology of Literature on Aging*. Ed. Margaret Cruikshank. Topsham, Maine: Just Write Books, 2006. P. 36-7.

Harris, Maria. *Jubilee Time: Celebrating Women, Spirit, and the Advent of Age.* New York: Bantam/Random House, 1995. P. 7-9.

The Magic of Crone-dom (P. 40)

Stauffer, Susan Ann. "Crones Counsel: A Unique Model for Re-Visioning the Aging Experience and Creating Empowerment-Oriented Community Among Elder Women." The Crones Counsel, 2008. www.cronescounsel.org.

Achieving Your Beautiful Face (P. 41)

Axton, Hoyt. "Sometimes It's Easy." Words and music by Hoyt Axton. Irving Music, 1975. Hal Leonard Corporation.

The Real You (P. 42-43)

Williams, Margery. *The Velveteen Rabbit: Or How Toys Become Real.* New York: Doubleday, 1922. P. 4-8.

"I Hope You Dance!" (P. 44-45)

Womack, Lee Ann. "I Hope You Dance." I Hope You Dance. Comp. Mark D. Sanders and Tia Sillers. MCA Nashville, 2000.

Photo by Deloria, Dennis. "Dancers of the Third Age." Used by permission of Dance Exchange, Inc. For further information visit www.danceexchange.org

Lerman, Liz. *Teaching Dance to Senior Adults.* Springfield, IL: Charles C. Thomas, 1984. P. 103.

You Are a Precious Child (P. 46-47)

Ehrmann, Max. "Desiderata." 1927.

Welcoming Your Inner Elder (P. 48-49)

Harris, Maria. *Jubilee Time: Celebrating Women, Spirit, and the Advent of Age.* New York: Bantam/Random House, 1995. P. xxvi.

Healing in Her Wings (P. 50-51)

McCloud, Shiloh Sophia. "Healing in Her Wings." *Color of Woman: A Coloring Book and Journal.* Berkeley: McCloud Press, 2004.

Surrendering What You Have Outgrown (P. 52-53)

Ehrmann, Max. "Desiderata." 1927.

Planting Your Own Carob Tree (P. 54-55)

Erikson, Erik H. *Identity: Youth and Crisis*. New York: W.W. Norton, 1968. P. 138-139.

Napping in God's Hands (P. 56-57)

Allen, Woody. "Death (A Play)." *Without Feathers*. New York: Random House, 1975. P. 99.

Eating Mangoes While Naked (P. 60)

SARK (Susan Ariel Rainbow Kennedy). *Eat Mangoes Naked*. New York: Fireside/ Simon & Schuster, 2001.

---. *Succulent Wild Woman*. New York: Fireside/Simon & Schuster, 2001.

Your Real Beauty (P. 61)

Williams, Margery. *The Velveteen Rabbit: Or How Toys Become Real*. New York: Doubleday, 1922. P. 8.

Choosing Optimism (P. 63)

Delaney, Sarah and A. Elizabeth, with Amy Hill Hearth. *Having Our Say: The Delany Sisters' First 100 Years*. New York: Kodansha, 1993. P. 129-130, 210.

Healing Through Insight (P. 64-65)

Interpretation of Geela Rayzel Raphael's translation of "Maariv." Ruach Hamidbar: A Community Prayer Book for the Sabbath. Phoenix, AZ: Spirit of the Desert, n.d.

To Everything There is a Season (P. 66-67)

Tolbert, Anne. "A Personal 'Seder' to Celebrate Aging." *A Heart of Wisdom: Making the Jewish Journey from Midlife Through the Elder Years*. Ed. Susan Berrin. Woodstock, VT: Jewish Lights, 1997. www.jewishlights.com. P. 284.

Shuttle, Penelope and Peter Redgrove. *The Wise Wound: Eve's Curse and Everywoman*. New York: Richard Marek, 1978.

Honoring Even Uncertainty (P. 69)

Cramer, Kathryn D. *Roads Home: Seven Pathways to Midlife Wisdom*. New York: William Morrow, 1995. P. 259.

Allen, Woody. Interview. *The Illustrated Woody Allen Reader*. Ed. Linda Sunshine. New York: Alfred A. Knopf, 1993. P. 250.

Schachter-Shalomi, Zalman and Ronald Miller. *From Age-ing to Sage-ing: A Profound New Vision of Growing Older*. New York: Grand Central/Hachette, 1995. P. 90.

You Are a Vital Piece of the Whole (P. 74-75)

Shapiro, Rami M. *Wisdom of the Jewish Sages: A Modern Reading of Pirke Avot*. New York: Bell Tower, 1993. P. viii.

The Power of Community (P. 76-77)

Holitzka, Klaus. "The Power of Community." *Power Mandalas*. New York: Sterling, 2000.

You Are a Masterpiece (P. 78-79)

Halprin, Anna. Foreword. *Teaching Dance to Senior Adults*. By Liz Lerman. Springfield, IL: Charles C. Thomas, 1984. P. vii-viii.

Daughters and Mothers (P. 82-83)

Harris, Maria. *Jubilee Time: Celebrating Women, Spirit, and the Advent of Age*. New York: Bantam/Random House, 1995. P. 89.

A Visit to Your Inner Elder (Tea and Cookies Optional!) (P. 84-84)

Schachter-Shalomi, Zalman and Ronald Miller. *From Age-ing to Sage-ing: A Profound New Vision of Growing Older*. New York: Grand Central/Hachette, 1995. P. 12, 16-17, 274-275.

Go Forth on the Quest (P. 86-87)

Waskow, Arthur Ocean and Phyllis Ocean Berman. *A Time for Every Purpose Under Heaven: The Jewish Life-Spiral as a Spiritual Path*. New York: Farrar, Straus and Giroux, 2002. P. 166.

Copyright Acknowledgments

If you would like additional copies of
Wise Older Woman: Growing Grace and Sass,
please visit wiseolderwoman.com.

Made in the USA
San Bernardino, CA
24 March 2014